PATTERNS IN THE SKY

THE MOON
and Its Patterns

by Thomas K. Adamson

PEBBLE
a capstone imprint

Published by Pebble, an imprint of Capstone.
1710 Roe Crest Drive, North Mankato, Minnesota 56003
capstonepub.com

Copyright © 2023 by Capstone. All rights reserved. No part of this publication may be reproduced in whole or in part, or stored in a retrieval system, or transmitted in any form or by any means, electronic, mechanical, photocopying, recording, or otherwise, without written permission of the publisher.

Library of Congress Cataloging-in-Publication Data is available on the Library of Congress website.
ISBN: 9781666355017 (hardcover)
ISBN: 9781666355055 (paperback)
ISBN: 9781666355093 (ebook PDF)

Summary: What is the moon? Why do we see it at night? And why does it seem to change shape? Learn the answers to these questions and more in this easy-to-read title and discover the science behind the moon and its patterns.

Editorial Credits
Editor: Alison Deering; Designer: Sarah Bennett; Media Researcher: Svetlana Zhurkin; Production Specialist: Katy LaVigne

Image Credits
Shutterstock: 3000ad, 4–5, AstroStar, 16, BlueRingMedia, 19, flashpict, 11, kaopanom, 15, Mike Pellinni, cover, pullia, 17, sdecoret, 9, SunflowerMomma, 18, Thitiwat Luechaudompan, 1, Tim Murphy, 6, Tom Reichner, 8, tomasandrascik, 10, Triff, 4 (top left) and throughout, udaix, 7, Viktor Klagyivik, 12–13; Svetlana Zhurkin: 20, 21

All internet sites appearing in back matter were available and accurate when this book was sent to press.

Table of Contents

What Are Moons? 4

Why Does the Moon Rise in One Place and Set in Another? 6

Why Does the Moon Change Shape? 8

What Are the Phases of the Moon? 10

How Often Does a Full Moon Happen? 12

Can We See the Moon During the Day? 14

Does the Moon Disappear? 16

Does the Moon Affect Us? 18

    Make Sweet Moon Phases 20

    Glossary 22

    Read More 23

    Internet Sites 23

    Index 24

    About the Author 24

Words in **bold** are in the glossary.

What Are Moons?

Moons are natural objects that move around **planets**. Earth has one moon. It is the brightest object in our sky other than the sun.

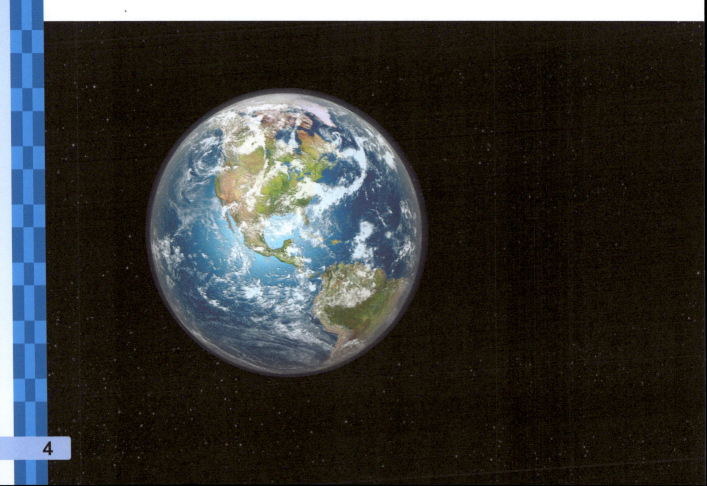

The moon is not always the same distance from Earth. On average, it is 238,855 miles (384,400 kilometers) away. That is about 30 Earths!

Why Does the Moon Rise in One Place and Set in Another?

Earth spins. That is what makes the moon rise and set. Because Earth rotates to the east, the moon moves across the sky from east to west.

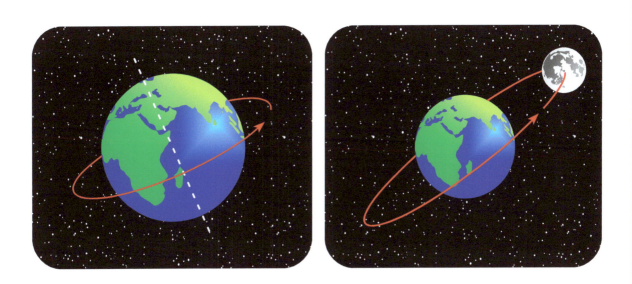

The moon also moves around Earth.
It moves in the same direction Earth spins.
The moon gets ahead of Earth's rotation.
That's why it rises about 50 minutes later each day.

Why Does the Moon Change Shape?

The moon itself doesn't change shape. But our view of the moon does change!

The moon does not make its own light. Sunlight bounces off the moon's surface, lighting up half of it. The other half is dark.

As the moon moves around Earth, how much of that bright side we see changes. We see this as the changing **phases** of the moon.

What Are the Phases of the Moon?

There are eight phases of the moon. During a **new moon**, the far side of the moon is lit. We can't see it from Earth.

A **crescent** moon is a curved sliver. A quarter moon looks like a half circle. The moon looks brighter during the **gibbous** phase.

PHASES OF THE MOON

new moon	crescent moon	quarter moon	gibbous moon |ри

full moon	gibbous moon	quarter moon	crescent moon

How Often Does a Full Moon Happen?

A **full moon** looks like a complete circle. The moon circles Earth once every 27 days. Because Earth is also spinning, the phases of the moon take a little longer. We see a full moon every 29.5 days.

Can We See the Moon During the Day?

Yes! But we might not notice it. A bright blue sky makes the moon hard to spot. It's easier to see the bright moon shining against the black night sky.

There is never a full moon in the daytime sky. The moon and sun are on opposite sides of Earth during a full moon.

15

Does the Moon Disappear?

No! But sometimes it looks like it. An **eclipse** happens when Earth's shadow covers the moon. During a total eclipse, the moon is completely covered.

In a partial eclipse, only part of the shadow lands on the moon. The shadow gradually grows. Then it goes away without completely covering the moon.

Does the Moon Affect Us?

The moon is far away. But its **gravity** tugs on Earth. It changes Earth's shape!

We notice this change most easily as **tides** along ocean beaches. Tides are the rising and falling of ocean levels caused by the moon.

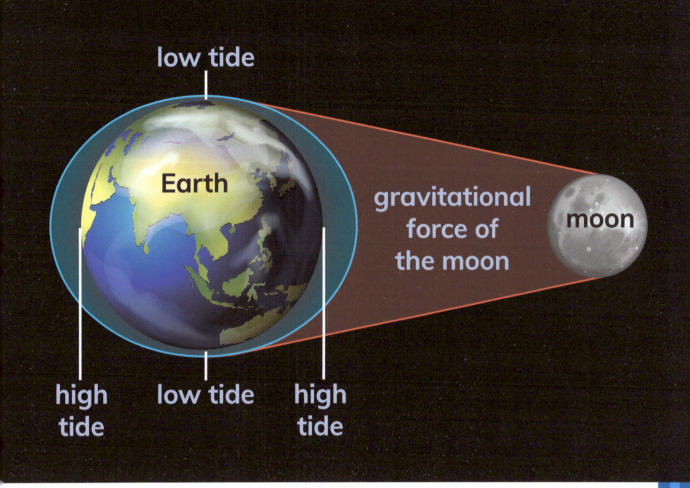

The moon's gravity tugs on the closest side of Earth. It also tugs on the side farthest away. That causes high tide. Low tide occurs on the other parts of Earth as it rotates.

Make Sweet Moon Phases

Use sandwich cookies to make the different phases of the moon!

What You Need

- 4-8 round sandwich cookies
- toothpick
- butter knife

What You Do

1. Carefully remove one side of the cookie from the frosting.

2. Use the toothpick to draw the shape of one moon phase in the frosting.

3. Use the butter knife to lift part of the frosting off the cookie. This empty part represents the dark side of the moon. The frosting that's left represents the bright part of the moon we see.

4. Create the rest of the moon phases with the other cookies.

Glossary

crescent (KRESS-uhnt)—a curved shape that looks like the moon when it is a sliver in the sky

eclipse (ih-KLIPS)—an event in which Earth's shadow passes over the moon or the moon's shadow passes over Earth

full moon (FUHL MOON)—the moon when it appears as a bright circle

gibbous (GIB-uhs)—when the lit part of the moon looks larger than a semicircle and smaller than a full circle

gravity (GRAV-uh-tee)—a force that pulls objects together

moon (MOON)—an object that moves around a planet

new moon (NOO MOON)—the moon's phase when its dark side is toward Earth

phase (FAZE)—a stage; the moon's phases are the shapes that it appears to take over a month

planet (PLAN-it)—a large object that moves around a star; Earth is a planet

tide (TIDE)—the daily rising and falling of the ocean level

Read More

Grack, Rachel. *Curious About the Moon.* Mankato, MN: Amicus Ink, 2022.

Roesser, Marie. *Why Does the Moon Change Shape?* New York: Gareth Stevens Publishing, 2021.

Waxman, Laura Hamilton. *Let's Explore Phases of the Moon.* Minneapolis: Lerner Publications, 2022.

Internet Sites

NASA Science: Moon in Motion
moon.nasa.gov/moon-in-motion/moon-phases

National Geographic Kids: The Phases of the Moon
natgeokids.com/uk/discover/science/space/the-phases-of-the-moon

SciJinks: What Causes Tides?
scijinks.gov/tides

Index

appearance, 4, 8–9, 10, 12, 14, 17

crescent moon, 10

distance, 5

Earth's movement, 6–7, 12

eclipses, 17

full moon, 12, 14

gibbous moon, 10

gravity, 18–19

moon phases, 9, 10, 12

new moon, 10

oceans, 18–19

phases of the moon, 14

quarter moon, 10

tides, 18–19

About the Author

Thomas K. Adamson has written lots of nonfiction books for kids. Sports, math, science, cool vehicles—a little of everything! When not writing, he likes to hike, watch movies, eat pizza, and of course, read. Tom lives in South Dakota with his wife, two sons, and a Morkie named Moe.